Titles by Janvier Chouteu-Chando

The Usurper: and Other Stories
Triple Agent, Double Cross
Disciples of Fortune
The Union Moujik
Splendid Comets
Flash of the Sun
Fortune Calls
Fortune's Master
Fortune's Children
The Norilsk Bears
To Be In Love and To Be Wise
The Fire and Ice Legend
The Sweetest Madness
The Grandmothers
The Hunger Fire
The Shades of Fire
Father and Sons
The Doctors
Dark Shades
Fateful Ties
The Verdict of Hades
His Majesty's Trial
Ngoko's Folly
The Usurper
The Dowry
I am Hated
The Oaf

Non-Fiction Titles by Janvier Chouteu-Chando
FALLEN HEROES: African Leaders Whose Assassinations…
BROKEN ENGAGEMENT: Why a Donald Trump Win…
THEIR LAST STAND: Donald Trump's Upset Victory…
Ukraine: The Tug-of-war between Russia and the West
THE CANARY IN A COAL MINE EFFECT:...
Cameroon: The Haunted Heart of Africa

The Fall of Blaise Compaore of Burkina Faso and the Anticipated Benefits for Africa

Janvier Tchouteu

TISI BOOKS

NEW YORK, RALEIGH, LONDON, AMSTERDAM

PUBLISHED BY TISI BOOKS
www.tisibooks.com

NEW YORK, RALEIGH, LONDON, AMSTERDAM

Printed in The United States of America

Acknowledgement

My sincerest, warmest, and everlasting thanks to all my family: special attributes to my mothers—Elizabeth Matsiliso and Theresia Njomo.

DEDICATION

This account is dedicated to the loving memory of
Dr. Samuel F. Tchwenko

The Fall of Blaise Compaore of Burkina Faso and the Anticipated Benefits for Africa

Contents

MAPS

Burkina Faso on a map of the world

Burkina Faso on a map of Africa

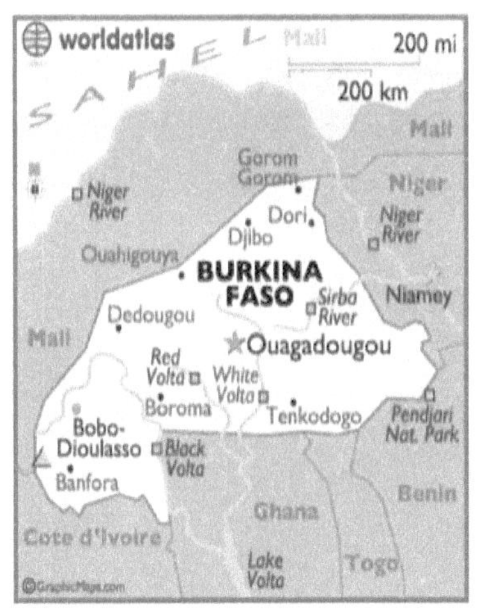

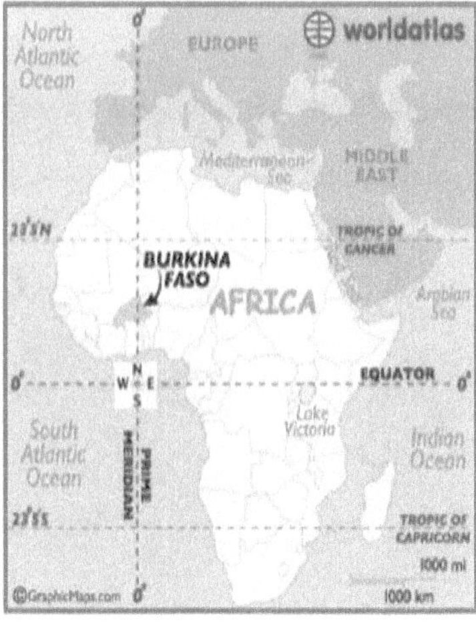

Partition map of Africa (1884-1914)

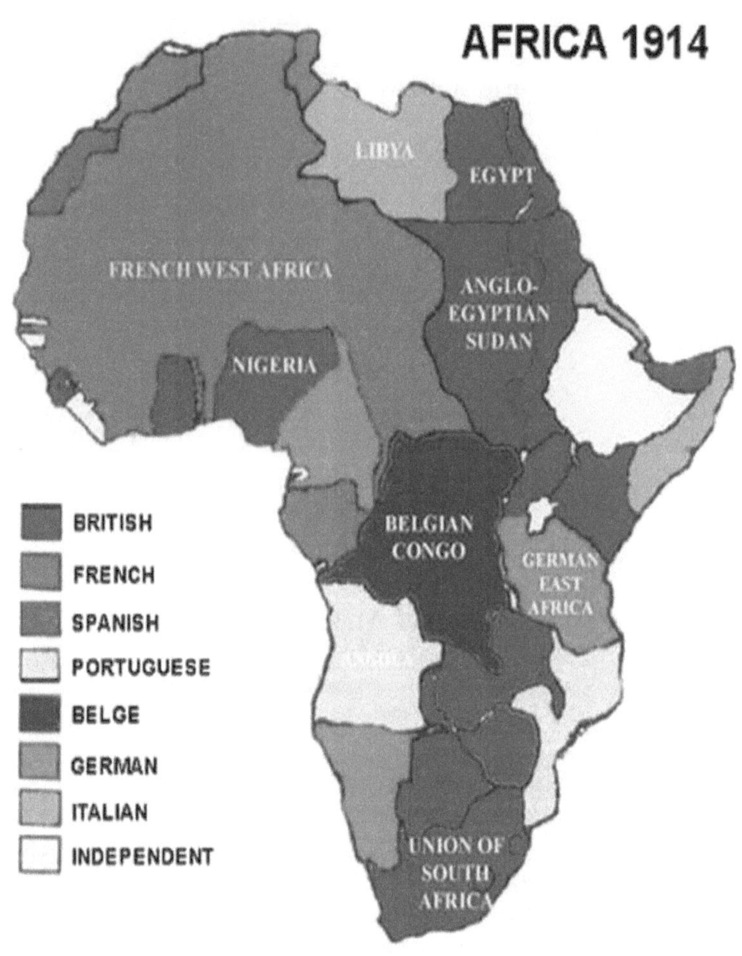

Political map of Africa

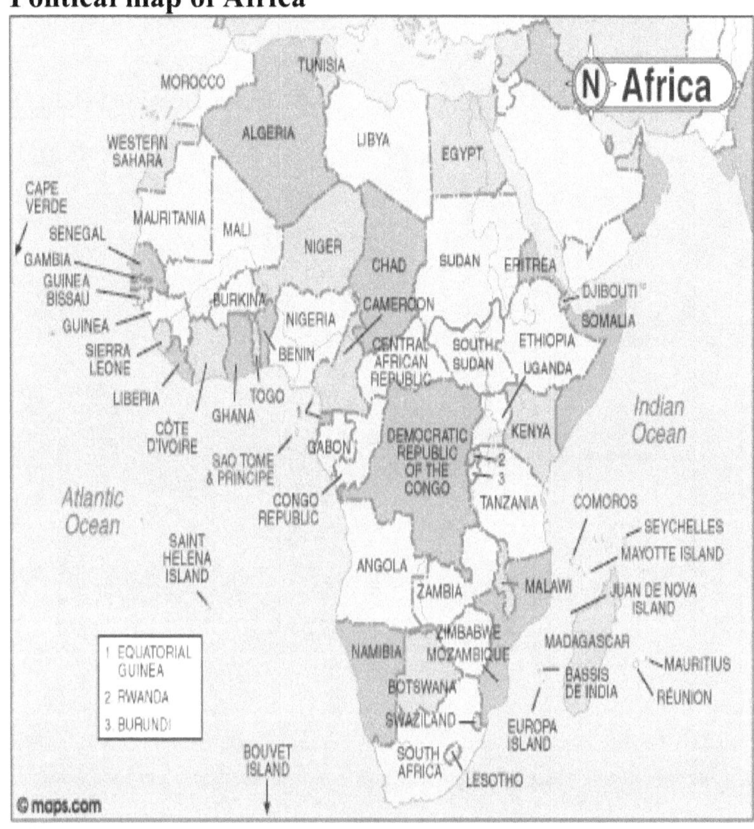

African Democracy Ratings

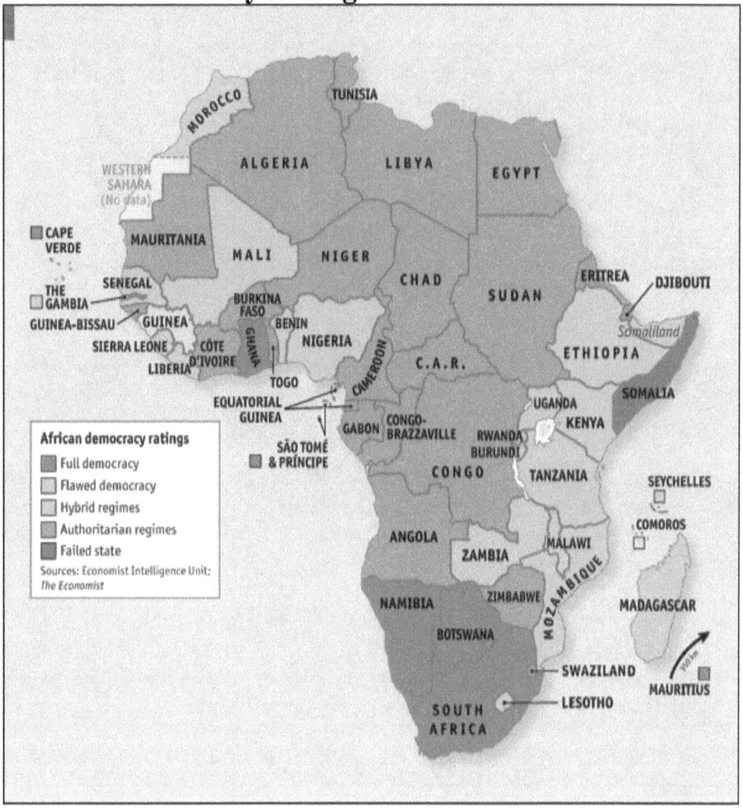

INTRODUCTION

It is difficult to get a clear cut answer explaining why people betray a cause, that is, by double-crossing someone or those they were involved in the cause with, and more especially by carrying out the destruction of people who put the general purpose of the cause far above their personal considerations, and who at no point in time thought of betraying those they are or were engaged in that cause with. When that cause goes beyond safeguarding the interests of the people it clearly stood out for, and even embraces the quest to serve all of humanity, those with a strong sense of conscience tend to be even more appalled by the betrayal.

In my search for the answer to why Burkina Faso is once again a major geopolitical flashpoint in the world, in my pry to know and to understand the reason(s) behind the extraordinary determination of the people of the Sahelian nation in West Africa who braved the odds and challenged an entrenched French-backed regime known for its bloody rule, I explored the assassination of Thomas Sankara, the ousted Blaise Compaore's predecessor, whom he killed. In my research and analysis, I arrived at a fascinating conclusion. The Sankara legacy would keep on summoning the people of Burkina Faso from his grave until a New Burkina Faso is established as the country of free, upright and self-reliant people, the New Burkina Faso that Sankara had in mind before he was assassinated.

The Sankara legacy is a force that cannot be suppressed for long and would keep on resurfacing in the course of the socio-economic and political development of Burkina Faso and Africa as they go through the bumps of history.

Chapter One

Blaise Compaore

At long last, Blaise Compaore, the cold-blooded dictator of Burkina Faso, is gone, even though he has been replaced by someone of the system that France put in place. Even so, the ultimate objective of Burkinabes should be to dismantle the system and replace it with something progressive that nullifies the enslaving Colonial Pact that the Fifth Republic France led by the legendary French general and statesman Charles De Gaulle forced France's former colonies and territories in Africa to sign before allowing them to become members of the United Nations Organization through the sham process of granting them independence. These Francophone countries of Africa still find themselves trapped in a neocolonialist setup that guarantees France's interest above the interests of others, even above the interest of the home country that is the subject matter.

It is close to seven decades that most of the territories in Africa colonized by France and Britain were granted their so-called independence. But what do we discover about the former French colonies in Africa fettered by the French-imposed agreements with social, economic and political components that virtually limit the independence of these countries? Everywhere in Francophone Africa are varying combinations of instability, autocracy, semi-democracies, liberal autocracy, democracy deficits, underdevelopment, poverty, illiteracy, crime, corruption, disease and despondence.

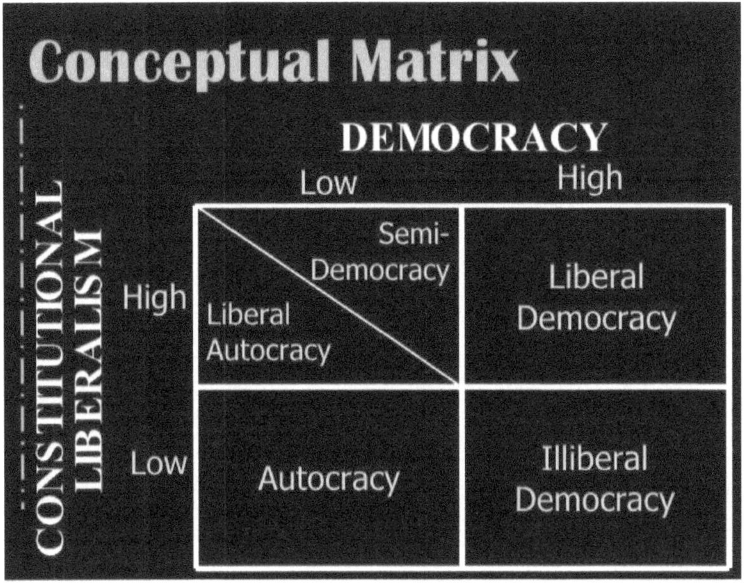

While bearing in mind the fact that the overriding objective in Burkina Faso at the moment is to create stability and dismantle the autocratic system France reimposed on this West African country after engineering the assassination of the incorruptible Thomas Sankara and his loyal associates by using the hand of Sankara's second in command, his close friend and confidante Blaise Compaore; the new political force in Burkina Faso should make as its primary and overriding long-term objective the establishment of structures that would ensure democracy, freedom, liberty, the rule of law, education, poverty reduction, transparency, economic progress, technological openness and fiscal responsibility for the country.

Chapter Two

Most of the citizens of Burkina Faso agree that the biggest political crime committed in the history of the country was the assassination of Thomas Sankara by his successor Blaise Compaore. Yes, Blaise Compaore made it to power almost three decades ago by killing the popular former president Sankara (he was very close to him) in a French-sponsored coup over claims that Sankara was a Marxist. It was treachery at its worst, an act that not only hurt Burkina Faso's self-reliant path pursued during the four years of the Sankara presidency, but that retarded the wind of change, which Sankara's uprightness, patriotism, pan-Africanism and openness was encouraging in Africa, a wind of change apparently made unstoppable by Mikhail Gorbachev's Glasnost and Perestroika that was making dictatorships, authoritarianism and totalitarianism redundant in the world.

Furthermore, not only did Sankara's death on October 15, 1987, aged thirty seven (37), result in the extirpation of youthful steam in African politics, it also emboldened the former colonial masters and their puppets to reverse the push for democracy in Africa and drove home the message to African leaders like Jerry Rawlings of Ghana who shared similar views to Sankara that they could be next in line for elimination if they stuck with their ideas of a future

Africa unshackled by foreign interests.

Almost three decades of Compaore rule has revealed that he reversed the political and social gains of Sankara's rule in favor of France, a turnaround that saw Burkina Faso going against its interest by honoring, once again, the lopsided agreement it signed with France in 1960 that completely made the West African nation a vassal of its former colonial master. In fact, it rejoined the club of Francophone African countries that were neocolonial appendages of France.

Burkina Faso's so-called benefits from this realignment during the twenty-seven (27) years that Compaore was in power are economic handouts that are making the country more reliant on France in the long run.

For Africa, Sankara's death not only traumatized the few African leaders that believed in genuine African unity, democracy, genuine African independence, an end to neocolonialism in the continent, the establishment of the rule of law in the different African countries, and in encouraging new commitments to safeguard and defend the interests of the continent and its constituent states; it discourage the young and enlightened Africans who had come to believe that the era of armed struggle to realize political change was over; and above all, it encouraged the neo-colonialists and their African puppets, most of whom have the evil disposition, to flagrantly pursue actions and policies that disregard human rights of Africans and that are devoid of planning, a sense of direction and benefits that would improve the welfare of the people.

In most countries in Francophone Africa, France and

some Western governments have installed their puppets who have been in power for decades, and who during their rules, have been impoverishing their people, selling off their country's resources, saving the wealth they loot from their home countries in foreign banks (Europe and the Americas in particular). They also use some of the stolen wealth in buying properties and businesses abroad (Paul Biya of Cameroon — 36 years, the Eyademas of Togo — 5 decades, the Bongos of Gabon — 5 decades, Denis Sassou Nguesso of Congo Brazzaville — three decades etc.).

It does not come as a surprise that the people are fed up with the paralysis in their home countries, which hardly anyone disagrees, is caused by political leaderships that don't have a clue of what good governance is all about and that have no idea of what it takes to move their countries forward into the 21st century by using the human and material resources of the countries they are misruling, as well as the levers of power they usurped, power that is actually supposed to be used to make it possible for hard-working citizens to live a decent life. These puppets are in power to safeguard the benefits France gets from its former colonies as spelled out in the "Colonial Pact", which France imposed on its colonies before granting them independence in the 1960s. Books like "Triple Agent Double Cross", "Disciples of Fortune" provide a better insight.

Chapter Three

While Burkina Faso would be remembered in African history, and more especially in Francophone African history as the first country where a Francophone African dictator was forced to step down due to a popular revolt by the masses he had been oppressing and suppressing with the help of foreign interest groups, especially the former colonial master, the events should be looked upon today as the precedence in the struggle to free Africa from tyranny, as a liberating fervor that would see the "Power of the People" confining other dictatorships like those of Paul Biya of Cameroon, the Eyademas of Togo, the Bongos of Gabon, the Kabilas of Congo-Kinshasa, Sasse Nguesso of Congo-Brazzaville, Obiang Nguema of Equatorial Guinea, Robert Mugabe of Zimbabwe, Isaias Afwerki of Eritrea, Omar Al-Bashir of Sudan, Idris Derby of Chad, Yahya Jammeh of Gambia, Yoweri Museveni of Uganda and other less vile figures in the African political scene to the dirt heaps of history.

Let us hope that African leaders who are not so vile will not turn into leeches like the aforementioned heads of state have become, while enjoying the tacit and open blessings of foreign entities, foreign powers who, in addition to safeguarding their selfish interests in their relations with these handicapped and evil dictators, could even be jubilant in thinking that these monsters calling themselves presidents or heads of state embody Africa and Africans.

The day that Paul Biya's 35-year reign, which France imposed on the Cameroonian people, will end and the anachronistic system of six decades that France imposed on Cameroon and the rest of French-speaking Africa will be dismantled, will be the beginning of true freedom, prosperity, and democracy in Francophone Africa.

Blaise Compaore was trying to emulate Paul Biya from Cameroon in his attempt to get around the two-term limit for the presidency of Burkina Faso, as set out in the constitution he approved a decade ago. He failed, but not Paul Biya from Cameroon did not. The Cameroonian president again changed his constitution in 2008, allowing him to get two more seven-year terms by holding elections that are nothing but masquerades and sacrilege for democracy, a farce he has always managed to accomplish with the open or tacit support of France, the Western Allies of France and other foreign interest groups who have always legitimized its usurpation with messages of congratulations for his victory, despite the fact that the elections were masquerades or mind-boggling farces. Even though the Cameroonian people protested and 150 were killed in February 2008, Paul Biya continued his plan and changed the constitution, then again falsified the elections in October 2011, after which he promised the Cameroonian people another victory in 2018, when he would be 85 years old. He has continued to impose himself on the people, with the support of France, the business world, and other Western governments. And today, Cameroon, one of Africa's richest countries resources-wise (human and material), is almost a bankrupt state with the highest brain drain rate in Africa and without a sense of direction.

In a world devoid of hypocrisy, human leeches like these psychopaths posing as African heads of state would not be tolerated by powers who brandish human values as the cornerstone of their advanced cultures or civilization. The time has come for the leaders of the civilized or cultured world to understand that their interests are best safeguarded in a world and more particularly in an Africa where the vast majority of the people have an interest in the progress of their countries.

Janvier Tchouteu is an Author, a political writer, and a pro-Democracy advocate. Some of his other works include "THE CANARY IN A COAL MINE EFFECT: Recent Political Assassinations That Transformed Countries, Regions and the World", "The Usurper: and Other Stories".

October 31, 2014